My PERSONAL PRAYER BOOK

ALVIN N. ROGNESS

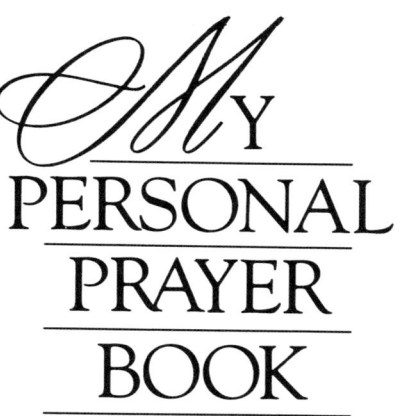

My PERSONAL PRAYER BOOK

AUGSBURG Publishing House • Minneapolis

MY PERSONAL PRAYER BOOK

Copyright © 1988 Augsburg Publishing House

All rights reserved. Except for brief quotations in critical articles or reviews, no part of this book may be reproduced in any manner without prior written permission from the publisher. Write to: Permissions, Augsburg Publishing House, 426 S. Fifth St., Box 1209, Minneapolis MN 55440.

Scripture quotations unless otherwise noted are from the Holy Bible: New International Version. Copyright 1978 by the New York International Bible Society. Used by permission of Zondervan Bible Publishers.

Library of Congress Cataloging-in-Publication Data

Rogness, Alvin N., 1906–
  My personal prayer book / Alvin N. Rogness.
    p.   cm.
  ISBN 0-8066-2358-6
  1. Prayers. 2. Prayer—Biblical teaching. 3. Bible—Criticism, interpretation, etc.   I. Title.
  BV260.R64   1988
  242'.8—dc19   88-28625
                                                                        CIP

Manufactured in the U.S.A.   APH 10-4599

    4 5 6 7 8 9 0 1 2 3 4 5 6 7 8 9

Contents

God Is with You	7
Using Your Bible	9
When You Pray	11
Some Thoughts on Prayer	13
When Whirlwinds Rage	17
When Jesus Comes Aboard	20
When Love Is Not Easy	22
Use Me, Lord	24
Keeping My Joy	26
Bless Us All	28
When I Worry	30
Let Me Rest in You	33
When Criticism Comes	35
Help Me Let the Wrongs Go	37
When I Feel Outdone	39
Come to Me	42
Hold My Hand	44
When I Need Proof	46

When God Seems Far Off	49
When Memories Trouble Me	50
When Tomorrow Looks Gloomy	51
When I Think of Dying	53
When I Want Wealth	54
When I Doubt	56
When I Can't Forgive Someone	57
When I Can't Forgive Myself	58
Finding Each Day's Joy	62

God is With You

God created you, loves you, and is always with you, no matter how difficult life seems to be. You may especially need to be assured this is true during times of crisis, disappointment, illness, or grief. When answers don't come easily, you are more likely to welcome a word from the Lord, a comforting word. In this book you will find brief reflections on a variety of themes, prayers, hymns, passages from the Bible, and quotations from other writings. May this book bring you hope and courage when you feel discouraged and heavyhearted.

E. Stanley Jones, great missionary to India, tells of an eagle suddenly caught in the fury of a mountain storm. The gale threatened to dash him against the boulders. He wheeled into the wind, tilted his wings at a certain angle, and the very winds that might have destroyed him lifted him upward, until at last he was above the storm. That's what can happen to you. You can adopt the attitude of faith and hope and patience, even cheerfulness. You can find new strength in prayer. Then times that threaten to discourage and crush you may do what the winds did for the eagle—lift you up to a new understanding, a new charity, a new peace.

When life becomes difficult, remember that you are carried along by all kinds of people who care including family and friends, and also professionals like doctors, pastors, and counselors. Through them, and behind them all, is a Lord who gave his life on a cross to forgive, to heal, and to hold you for life and eternity. Knowing this can be the first step in finding the strength and comfort God intends for you.

Using Your Bible

Most of us in our busy, daily lives have not read the Bible very much. More than any other book in the world, it has given hope and comfort in time of need. It has changed the lives of more people than all other books combined. In a strange way, God hides in the Bible and when we read the book, he finds his way into our minds and hearts. Now may be a good time to become more familiar with it.

To start with, read Psalm 23, then Psalms 19, 46, 51, 90, 91, 103, 121, and 130. After the Psalms, go to Isaiah and read Chapters 40, 53, and 55.

Going to the New Testament, you may

want to read one of the Gospels from beginning to end. Try the Gospel of John. It won't take you much more than an hour and a half. Among the epistles, try Romans 8; Romans 12; 1 Corinthians 13; Ephesians 6:10-20; Philippians 3:4-9; and Hebrews 12:1-17. There may be other passages which on your own you have found helpful. Some all-time favorite Bible passages are even printed in full in this book; you will discover them as you read. There are so many places where God speaks directly to us; these suggestions are but a beginning.

HEN YOU PRAY

When you pray you are talking to God. You have never seen or heard or touched him. But you talk to him as you would talk to a friend in the same room with you. He has invited us to ask for anything we like.

If God loves us, and if he knows better than we ourselves what we need, why bother him with prayers? Does he hold back, waiting for us to ask, before he gives what we need? Of course not. But he wants us to talk to him. He would be a strange Father if he wanted us to keep still and never talk to him.

When we start by asking him for things we need, we soon discover we're also thanking God for what we have—friends and family, eyes to see with, minds that can understand, a free country. It can be a long list.

God also invites us to pray for others. Think of them, one by one, and pray for them. Who knows what blessings reach them through our prayers.

God is not like a newspaper carrier who places the paper at your door and leaves. God gives gifts, and then stays. Prayer is one way of inviting God in. We can well start with the prayer Jesus himself taught us.

> Our Father, who art in heaven,
>   Hallowed by Thy name.
> Thy kingdom come,
>   Thy will be done on earth as it is in heaven.
> Give us this day our daily bread,
>   And forgive us our trespasses, as we forgive those who trespass against us.
> And lead us not into temptation,
>   But deliver us from evil.
> For Thine is the kingdom, and the power and the glory, for ever and ever. Amen.

Some Thoughts on Prayer

Some prayers are answered in deep love because they are not answered. . . . There are two ways to remove a burden: one is to banish the load, the other is to double the strength.

George A. Buttrick

"For my thoughts are not your thoughts,
 neither are your ways my ways,"
  declares the Lord.
"As the heavens are higher than the earth,
 so are my ways higher than your ways
 and my thoughts than your thoughts."
Isaiah 55:8-9

God answers prayer; sometimes, when hearts
 are weak,

He gives the very gifts believers seek.
But often faith must learn a deeper rest;
And trust God's silence when he does not speak;
For he whose Name is Love will send the best.
Stars may burn out, nor mountain walls endure,
But God is true, his promises are sure.
Author unknown

He asked for strength that he might achieve;
    He was made weak that he might obey.
He asked for health that he might do greater things;
    He was given infirmity that he might do better things.
He asked for riches that he might be happy;
    He was given poverty that he might be wise.
He asked for power that he might have the praise of men;
    He was given weakness that he might feel the need of God.

He asked for all things that he might enjoy life;
> He was given life that he might enjoy all things.

He has received nothing that he asked for;
> All that he hoped for. His prayer is answered.

He is most blessed.

Author unknown

Do you not know?
> Have you not heard?

The Lord is the everlasting God,
> the Creator of the ends of the earth.

He will not grow tired or weary,
> and his understanding no one can fathom.

He gives strength to the weary
> and increases the power of the weak.

Even youths grow tired and weary,
> and young men stumble and fall;

but those who hope in the Lord
> will renew their strength.

They will soar on wings like eagles;
> they will run and not grow weary,
> they will walk and not be faint.
>> *Isaiah 40:28-31*

WHEN WHIRLWINDS RAGE

They sow the wind and reap the whirlwind.
Hosea 8:7a

Do not be deceived: God cannot be mocked. A man reaps what he sows.
Galatians 6:7

We hear voices of doom on every hand, O Lord. The whirlwind is rolling toward us. The bomb hangs over us, air and water are polluted, hunger stalks a third of the world, a plague may be on the way.

What do we do with these voices, Lord? It seems to me that even among Christians there are three possible ways to go. The first, *abject pessimism*. Things have gotten out of hand and we on this "late, great planet earth" can only wait for the storms that will sweep everything away. Second, *naive optimism* that rests easy because "things have been bad before, and somehow we have muddled through." Both of these attitudes must be wrong, Lord, because they leave us doing nothing.

The third is *hope*. You did put the management of the planet in our hands, didn't you? No matter how dark the future may appear, you tell us to keep working "while it is day." You have ordered us to have hope, even when everything looks hopeless. With you on hand to forgive, to correct, to guide, and to inspire and empower, who are we, Lord, to say that nothing can or need be done? Surely you don't want us to give up on this world you love and called good.

Unexpected storms do strike. You, Lord, were with our family the night when, after a car accident, policemen came to our door asking if Paul was our son. You are with your children when the doctor's verdict is cancer. You are there in floods, drought, earthquakes. If we do unleash a nuclear holocaust, even then you will not give up on us. If we burn down the house you have provided for us here, you have a better home in store, a heavenly one. Thanks, God, that even in the whirlwind, your everlasting mercy will hold us fast.

WHEN JESUS COMES ABOARD

Lord, you said the Father in heaven knows when a sparrow falls to the ground. Help me believe you are concerned not only with the sparrows but with each of us in our doubts and troubles.

I remember all too well the bitter discoveries I have made when I have tried to run my own life in my own way, when I try to steer my ship with no help. Will you come aboard, Lord Jesus, and set a true course? If I have sailed off course, help me to find again the course that leads out of the storms toward the safe harbor.

I pray in that name which is above every name, in the name of Jesus Christ, my Lord. Amen.

A furious squall came up, and the waves broke over the boat, so that it was nearly swamped. Jesus was in the stern, sleeping on a cushion. The disciples woke him and said to him, "Teacher, don't you care if we drown?" He got up, rebuked the wind and said to the waves, "Quiet! Be still!" Then the wind died down and it was completely calm. He said to his disciples, "Why are you so afraid? Do you still have no faith?" They were terrified and asked each other, "Who is this? Even the wind and the waves obey him!"

Mark 4:37-41

WHEN LOVE IS NOT EASY

For this reason I kneel before the Father, from whom his whole family in heaven and on earth derives its name.
Ephesians 3:14-15

Dear Lord, I grew up in a small town where everyone was of the same ethnic group, belonged to the same church, and supported the same political party. There was no need to love "other kinds" of people.

I have now seen a little of our plural world. I'm wondering, Lord, if it is as easy to love a black, an oriental, or an American Indian as it is to love someone like me. I think it is. We now have grandchildren with mixed racial backgrounds. In loving them we are learning to love a whole different race. We do have biases, Lord, and we need your help to surmount them.

Lord, not everyone in our town loved one another, though they had blood and religion in common. Petty rivalries, envy, and suspicion troubled us. Of course love was there too. Would it have been different if our village was thoroughly mixed?

We're trying hard as a church, Lord. You want us to be united in love for one another, but you do not want us to be some homogeneous mass or herd. Help us to enrich our church by opening doors to all.

Can we really love one another at all without your help? We are all terribly self-oriented. To forget self in love of one another may always be one of your miracles, even love between wife and husband and children.

Help us cross all borders with your love in our hearts.

There is neither Jew nor Greek, slave nor free, male nor female.
Galatians 3:28

Use Me, Lord

Lord, make us instruments of your peace.
  Where there is hatred, let us sow love;
  where there is injury, pardon;
  where there is discord, union;
  where there is doubt, faith;
  where there is despair, hope;
  where there is darkness, light;
  where there is sadness, joy.
Grant that we may not so much seek
  to be consoled as to console;
  to be understood as to understand;
  to be loved as to love.
For it is in giving that we receive;
  it is in pardoning that we are pardoned;
  and it is in dying that we are born to
    eternal life.

St. Francis of Assisi

For God so loved the world that he gave his one and only Son, that whoever believes in him shall not perish but have eternal life. For God did not send his Son into the world to condemn the world, but to save the world through him.

John 3:16-17

KEEPING MY JOY

You prepare a table before me in the presence of my enemies.

Psalm 23:5a

In the thick of the world's troubles, you still want us to have joy. You throw a party (prepare a table) even though dangers lurk around every corner.

Is it right for me to enjoy a good dinner when a third of the world is underfed? Some of my friends have gone through the pain of divorce; shall I let their sadness rob me of the sheer joy of our marriage?

Paul tells us "whatever is true, whatever is noble, whatever is right, whatever is pure, whatever is lovely, whatever is admirable

. . . think about such things." Isn't he telling us to turn our minds from the sordid acts and the violence that fill the newspapers and television and to bask in what is good?

There is much good. Help us make lists of all your blessings and keep our eyes on them. First, there is yourself, Lord. If nothing else, that should be enough. "Rejoice in the Lord always," said Paul, and added, "Present your requests to God." You must have a whole catalog of additional joys waiting for us.

The list can be long, Lord: a trip to visit friends, family, celebrations, nature's scenery, children, pets. There is this world of color, form, and music. We have a country where freedoms are protected. Do you want me to keep on listing?

With every item, help me joyfully give thanks.

BLESS US ALL

Watch thou, dear Lord, with those who wake, or watch, or weep tonight, and give thine angels charge over those who sleep. Tend thy sick ones, Lord Christ. Rest thy weary ones. Bless thy dying ones. Soothe thy suffering ones. Pity thine afflicted ones. Shield thy joyous ones. And all, for thy love's sake. Amen.

St. Augustine

The Lord is my shepherd, I shall not be in
    want.
    He makes me lie down in green pas-
        tures,
he leads me beside quiet waters,
    he restores my soul.

He guides me in paths of righteousness
>for his name's sake.
Even though I walk
>through the valley of the shadow of death,
I will fear no evil,
>for you are with me;
your rod and your staff,
>they comfort me.
You prepare a table before me
>in the presence of my enemies.
You anoint my head with oil;
>my cup overflows.
Surely goodness and love will follow me
>all the days of my life,
and I will dwell in the house of the Lord
>forever.

Psalm 23

WHEN I WORRY

Therefore I tell you, do not worry about your life, what you will eat or drink; or about your body, what you will wear. Is not life more important than food, and the body more important than clothes? . . . your heavenly Father knows that you need them.

Matthew 6:25,32

My fears and anxieties are a sin against you, aren't they, God? You know how hard it is for me to trust you for everything, not just for heaven, but for everything.

I know you love me. The cross is my ultimate assurance. I also know that you want the best for me; and that you know better than I what that best should be. Why then should I worry?

You understand. In the psalmist's words, "He knows how we are formed, he remembers that we are dust." But even if you do understand and are patient, our mistrust is still an offense, and must grieve you.

When I think of all the things that have worried me at one time or another and that never materialized, I am ashamed. In my anxieties I have robbed myself, my friends, and dear ones of the cheer that we all should have claimed from you.

Things go wrong, Lord. The world is full of dire possibilities. I would be a naive romantic to deny this. Isaiah said thick darkness would cover the earth. But he also said the light has come. He must have meant you, Jesus. Help us to know that however dark our journey may seem, you are there with us.

You knew anxieties too, didn't you, Lord? In the Garden of Gethsemene that fateful night, you were deeply troubled over what the morning would bring. But you didn't collapse in fear, or let bitterness overtake you. You put your own will into the will of God, your Father.

Isn't that what you want us to do? Help us to package all our worries and give them to you.

LET ME REST IN YOU

O father, thou art my eternity.
Not on the clasp of consciousness—on thee
My life depends; so thou remember, Lord.
In thee I rest; in sleep thou dost me fold;
In thee I labor; still in thee, grow old;
And dying, shall I not in thee, my life, be bold.

>   Diary of an Old Soul, *MacDonald*

I lift up my eyes to the hills—
>   where does my help come from?
My help comes from the Lord,
>   the Maker of heaven and earth.
He will not let your foot slip—
>   he who watches over you will not slumber;

indeed, he who watches over Israel
> will neither slumber nor sleep.

The Lord watches over you—
> the Lord is your shade at your right
> > hand;

the sun will not harm you by day,
> nor the moon by night.

The Lord will keep you from all harm—
> he will watch over your life;

the Lord will watch over your coming and
> > going
> both now and forevermore.

Psalm 121

WHEN CRITICISM COMES

> I care very little if I am judged by you or by any human court; indeed, I do not even judge myself. . . . It is the Lord who judges me. Therefore judge nothing before the appointed time; wait til the Lord comes.
> *1 Corinthians 4:3, 4b-5a*

Was Paul really troubled by what people thought of him, Lord? Most of us are much too troubled. We know quite well that if we're always wondering what people are saying about us, we only make ourselves unhappy. Paul was aware that most of the Pharisees thought him a traitor for following Jesus. Even among his fellow believers he was thought to be much too liberal with the Gentile Christians.

I confess I am eager to have people approve of me, Lord, but I also know that if I'm always doing and saying what people like, just to get their praise, I will be both dull and dishonest. If you had done that, you could have escaped the cross.

Every human court will make mistakes. Whether we are being judged or whether we are doing the judging, we will need caution. You told us not to judge, so that we would not be judged.

On the other hand, you have given us the gift of conscience. You expect us to make judgments about what's right and wrong. Even so, in dealing with others you want us to put the best construction on what they say and do.

You alone know the motives of our hearts, and you alone can give the final verdict. Give us the courage to seek and do your will and not worry so much about what people think.

HELP ME LET THE WRONGS GO

Make my forgiveness downright—such as I
Should perish if I did not have from thee;
I let the wrong go, withered up and dry.
Cursed with divine forgetfulness in me.
'Tis but self-pity, pleasant, mean, and sly,
Low whispering bids the paltry memory live;
What am I brother for, but to forgive!
      Diary of an Old Soul, *MacDonald*

This is the message we have heard from him and declare to you: God is light; in him is no darkness at all. If we claim to have fellowship with him yet walk in darkness, we lie and do not live by the truth. But if we walk in the light, as he is in the light, we have fellowship with one another, and the blood of Jesus, his Son, purifies us from all sin. If we claim to be without sin, we deceive ourselves and the truth is not in us. If we confess our sins, he is faithful and just and will forgive us our sins and purify us from all unrighteousness. If we claim we have not sinned, we make him out to be a liar and his word has no place in our lives.

1 John 1:5-10

WHEN I FEEL OUTDONE

What good is it for a man to gain the whole world, yet forfeit his soul?

Mark 8:36

Is it true, Lord, that in our culture we've got to be winners in order to feel successful? And that the price we pay for being winners is loneliness? Is it also true that if being first means everything to us, we cannot be happy when someone else wins? We can't rejoice with those who rejoice?

It probably isn't true that everyone loves a winner. Maybe it's easier to love a loser, because there are so many of us. It must be lonely at the top.

You, O Lord, have given us the certain cure for loneliness: be a servant! Stop this competition for preeminence. Lose yourselves in the sorrows and joys of others. In your own tireless concern for the needs of others, you showed us the way.

There must be lonely people, Lord, who wonder if anyone cares for them. They should know you love them, but maybe they have never heard of you. Are they trapped in an uncaring world?

They need not be, if they will follow your way. In that charming story of the Good Samaritan, you told the lawyer not to worry about who is his neighbor, but that he should be trying to be a neighbor to others.

If we set out to meet the needs of others, can we ever be lonely again? There are no limits to what doors may open. You have been the clue. To become a friend is more important than to find a friend. To love is more important than to be loved. To serve is more blessed than to be served.

It really isn't very important whether we

win or lose, is it, Lord? In a profound sense, we have already won. You have won a kingdom for us. And within that kingdom, you have given us the secret of joy. To serve you and others is the end of loneliness.

But thanks be to God! He gives us the victory through our Lord Jesus Christ.
1 Corinthians 15:57

Come to Me

Come to me, Lord: I will not speculate how,
Nor think at which door I would have thee
   appear,
Nor put off calling till my floors be swept,
but cry, "Come, Lord, come any way, come
   now."
Doors, windows, I throw wide, my head I
   bow,
and sit like someone who so long has slept
That he knows nothing till his life draw near.
   Diary of an Old Soul, *MacDonald*

   Come to me, all you who are weary and
burdened, and I will give you rest. Take my
yoke upon you and learn from me, for I am
gentle and humble in heart, and you will
find rest for your souls. For my yoke is easy
and my burden is light.

Matthew 11:28-30

Here I am! I stand at the door and knock. If anyone hears my voice and opens the door, I will come in and eat with him, and he with me.

Revelation 3:20

Hold My Hand

I was like Peter when he began to sink.
To Thee a new prayer therefore I have got—
That, when Death comes in earnest to my
 door,
And lead him to my room, up to my cot,
Then hold thy child's hand, hold and leave
 him not,
Till Death has done with him forevermore.
            Diary of an Old Soul, *MacDonald*

    What, then, shall we say in response to this? If God is for us, who can be against us? . . . For I am convinced that neither death nor life, neither the present nor the future, nor any powers, neither height nor depth, nor anything else in all creation, will be able to separate us from the love of God that is in Christ Jesus our Lord.

Romans 8:31,38-39

WHEN I NEED PROOF

But [Thomas] said to them, "Unless I see the nail marks in his hands . . . I will not believe it. . . ." Then Jesus told him, . . . "blessed are those who have not seen and yet have believed."

John 20:25,29

Why did Thomas doubt you had risen from the dead? Was it not, Lord, because he wanted so very much to believe you had? So, doubt can't always be bad. Had you not appeared to the other disciples, wouldn't they too have doubted?

For almost 2000 years now no one has seen you, yet hundreds of millions believe. We believe without having seen. But doubts do come. You have given us the Holy Spirit to help us to believe. Without the Spirit's help we would be in deep trouble.

Perhaps the hardest to believe is that you love us so much that you gave your life on a cross for us. Who are we to deserve such love from you who have all power in heaven and on earth? Occasionally, Lord, a terrible thought comes over me: what if the whole, wonderful story of the Bible is just a fairy tale? This doesn't happen often, fortunately. When it does, I become dreadfully lonely.

You have promised to be with us always. When we meet adversities, sickness, loss of friends and family, unemployment, can we trust that you have not forgotten us? I know we can.

I have been helped by theologian Soren Kierkegaard's 70,000 fathoms of water example. He said faith is like swimming in water that deep. No matter how long we swim, the bottom will never come up so we can lie on something solid and simply go through the motions of swimming. Until the end we will be swimming in 70,000 fathoms of water. Our faith is like that. We believe without resting firmly on what we can see and touch.

I keep my eyes on you, O Lord. If I don't, like Peter who began to sink when he took his eyes off you, I begin to drift. Help me so that, in all the storms and uncertainties of life, I may never lose sight of you.

WHEN GOD SEEMS FAR OFF

Dear God, how do I get you into my room? I pray, but don't get any surge of feeling. When I read the Bible, do you get out of the pages into my heart? You have promised to hear, but where are you—out among the galaxies somewhere? I need you right here. I simply have to believe you are here because you said you would be. Amen.

And surely I am with you always, to the very end of the age.

Matthew 28:20b

WHEN MEMORIES TROUBLE ME

Lord, I wish I could forget a lot of things. I feel sorry for the many kind things I might have said and done, but didn't. You said you would both forgive and forget. The things I can't change, you've told me to forget. Help me do that. Amen.

He does not treat us as our sins deserve
> or repay us according to our iniquities.

For as high as the heavens are above the earth,
> so great is his love for those who fear him;

as far as the east is from the west,
> so far has he removed our transgressions from us.   *Psalm 103:10-12*

WHEN TOMORROW LOOKS GLOOMY

Dear God, how much of tomorrow do you want me to carry today? You told us not to be anxious about tomorrow. Does that mean that I can package all my worries and hopes and simply give them to you? Somehow I can handle today. If you will take charge of my tomorrow, I'll be glad. Amen.

As a father has compassion on his children,
    so the Lord has compassion on those
        who fear him;
for he knows how we are formed,
    he remembers that we are dust.
As for man, his days are like grass,

he flourishes like a flower of the field;
the wind blows over it and it is gone,
    and its place remembers it no more.
But from everlasting to everlasting
    the Lord's love is with those who fear
        him,
    and his righteousness with their
        children's children—
with those who keep his covenant
    and remember to obey his precepts.

Psalm 103:13-18

WHEN I THINK OF DYING

Dear Lord, I feel my heart beating, but as Longfellow says, "Our hearts, though stout and brave, still like muffled drums, are beating funeral marches to the grave." Do you want me to think of dying? I think you do. But you have told us not to be troubled, because you have gone on to prepare a room for us, and will come to get us when our time has come. Help me to think of death not so much as the end, but as the beginning of a wonderful life with you and with dear friends who already are with you. Amen.

We know that in all things God works for the good of those who love him, who have been called according to his purpose.
Romans 8:28

WHEN I WANT WEALTH

Do not store up for yourselves treasures on earth, where moth and rust destroy, and where thieves break in and steal. But store up for yourselves treasures in heaven. . . . For where your treasure is, there your heart will be also.

Matthew 6:19-21

I think I know how to do this, Lord, but I'm not sure. You died so we don't have to pay anything to be on good terms with you. It is the Father's good pleasure to give us the kingdom. You have given us the gospel. There is nothing left for us to do, is there? You do it all.

I can understand your caution about laying up treasures on earth. When the stock market crashed in 1929, people who thought they were wealthy found themselves overnight with paper of no value. In the 1970s and 1980s people who bought land at inflated values, in a few months saw land values shrink and their wealth slip away.

You want us to be prudent with money and property you entrust to us. You told us to care for our families, our own. But you also have a special stake in the poor, the homeless, the hungry, the disenfranchised. To invest in their welfare, is this not to lay up treasures in heaven?

And you must mean your church. Who else but we, the believers, are the people who must make sure the glorious gospel of the kingdom is made known the world over?

Fill our hearts with thanksgiving. Educate our minds to see the opportunities for doing your work. Take away the fears and anxieties that block us from being bold in laying up the treasures that belong to heaven.

WHEN I DOUBT

Dear God, sometimes doubts creep in. Do you really love me? Did you really die for me? Sometimes I wonder if you exist at all. Are you angry when I doubt? Haven't you promised to accept us just as we are, with all our weaknesses and doubts? You accept us for Jesus' sake, don't you, not because we have such wonderful faith? Amen.

Therefore, there is now no condemnation for those who are in Christ Jesus.
Romans 8:1

WHEN I CAN'T FORGIVE SOMEONE

Dear Lord, do you really mean I should forgive as you forgive? You told Peter that seven times was not enough: 70 times 7, you said. Could a Jewish man forgive those who killed his whole family in a gas chamber? Can a wife forgive a husband who beat her and who abandoned her? Being weighed down with bitterness and hatred gives no joy. I wish I could unload it all in one big act of forgiveness, but can I? You forgave the very people who crucified you. Help me forgive. Amen.

Jesus said, "Father, forgive them, for they do not know what they are doing."

Luke 23:34

WHEN I CAN'T FORGIVE MYSELF

Dear Lord, when you forgive me, does it make you sad when I can't forgive myself? When you wipe the slate clean for me, is it right for me to keep dredging up the guilt that you already have removed? Am I pleasing you by remembering, or do I please you by forgiving myself and forgetting? Help me to take your forgiveness seriously and find the joy of your salvation by forgiving myself too. Amen.

Blessed is he
    whose transgressions are forgiven,
    whose sins are covered.
Blessed is the man

whose sin the Lord does not count
    against him
and in whose spirit is no deceit.
When I kept silent,
    my bones wasted away
    through my groaning all day long.
For day and night
    your hand was heavy upon me;
my strength was sapped
    as in the heat of summer.
Then I acknowledged my sin to you
    and did not cover up my iniquity.
I said, "I will confess
    my transgressions to the Lord"—
and you forgave
    the guilt of my sin.

Psalm 32:1-5

God, give us grace to accept with serenity the things that cannot be changed, courage to change the things that can be changed, and the wisdom to distinguish the one from the other.

Reinhold Niebuhr

Thank you, Lord, for your grace:

Amazing grace! How sweet the sound
   that saved a wretch like me!
I once was lost, but now am found;
   Was blind, but now I see.

Through many dangers, toils and snares
   I have already come;
'Tis grace has brought me safe thus far
   and grace will lead me home.

For your comfort:

Thy holy wings, dear Savior,
Spread gently over me;
And thru the long night watches,
I'll rest secure in thee.
Whatever may betide me,
Be thou my hiding place,
And let me live and labor,
each day, Lord, by thy grace.

Thy pardon, Savior, grant me,
And cleanse me in thy blood:
Give me a willing spirit,

A heart both clean and good.
O take into thy keeping
Thy children, great and small,
And, while we sweetly slumber,
Enfold us, one and all. Amen.

Linda Sandell (1832-1903)

And for your blessing:

The Lord bless you
    and keep you;
the Lord make his face shine upon you
    and be gracious to you:
the Lord turn his face toward you,
    and give you peace.

Numbers 6:24-26

FINDING EACH DAY'S JOY

Let your eyes rest on your misfortunes, and you risk bitterness; if on your blessings, you invite gratitude. If you eye your neighbors' good fortune, you may be tempted to envy; if you focus on their need, you could be stirred to compassion and works of mercy—and to unexpected sources of joy.

Jesus gives us the clue to the whole matter of life's meaning. To be a servant, he said, is to find fulness. To zero in on one's own gain or safety is a dead-end street. To be sure, there are satisfactions in being a winner, but not the deep, pervading joy God designed us to find. The person who builds a prosperous business will be gratified with its annual profits, but his deeper joy will be in providing commodities that people need, in dealing sensitively with his employees, in supporting church and community causes, in having a loving family and cherished friends. In Dickens' *Christmas Carol*, Jacob Marley, the returned ghost, laments his misdirected life, "The dealings of my trade were but a drop in the comprehensive ocean of my business."

You will find joy at the end of each day as you make two quick inventories:

What blessings has God given me this day?

What people have I reached out to help today?

What blessings? Life itself is one; you have been given another day. You have talents to offer to the possibilities of this day. You have a brain that can think and dream. You have family and friends who love you. Most of all, you have assurance, in Christ, of God's constant and unending love.

What people? Many have crossed your path. Did you add to their cheer? Were you sensitive to their needs? Did you go out of your way to add a word of kindness, send a letter, make a phone call—some little token to brighten someone's day? In serving others we find the hidden treasures of the kingdom.

Thank you Lord, for listening to my reflections and prayers. Everything seems better when I talk with you, even though the way is not yet clear. But you are at my side to guide, correct, forgive, and comfort. When the dry seasons come and my heart is heavy or indifferent, at such times above all do not cast me from your presence. Bring me out of those moments into the joy and merriment of your kingdom. Thank you, thank you Lord!